T0246649

THE
STOIC
MINDSET

THE
STOIC
MINDSET

LIVING THE
TEN PRINCIPLES
OF STOICISM

MARK TUITERT

Translation by Haico Kaashoek

ST. MARTIN'S
ESSENTIALS
NEW YORK

Published in the United States by St. Martin's Essentials, an imprint
of St. Martin's Publishing Group

THE STOIC MINDSET. Copyright © 2024 by Mark Tuitert. Translation copyright
© 2024 by Haico Kaashoek. All rights reserved. Printed in the United States
of America. For information, address St. Martin's Publishing Group, 120
Broadway, New York, NY 10271.

www.stmartins.com

Designed by Ruben Steeman / buro RuSt

Written with the help of Thomas Hogeling

The Library of Congress Cataloging-in-Publication Data is available upon
request.

ISBN 978-1-250-32527-3 (hardback)
ISBN 978-1-250-29081-6 (ebook)

Our books may be purchased in bulk for promotional, educational, or business use. Please contact your local bookseller or the Macmillan Corporate
and Premium Sales Department at 1-800-221-7945, extension 5442, or by
email at MacmillanSpecialMarkets@macmillan.com.

Originally published as *Drive* in the Netherlands by Maven Publishing
in 2021

First U.S. Edition: 2024

10 9 8 7 6 5 4 3 2 1

CONTENTS

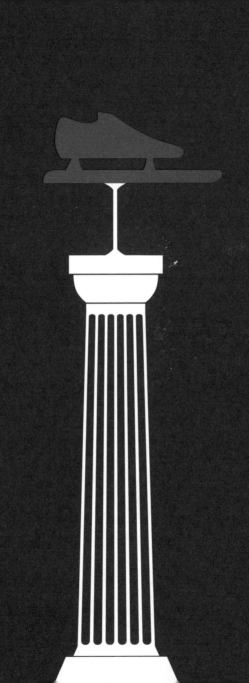

Introduction

Twelve years. I've trained twelve years for less than two minutes of speed skating. It's February 2010, and in two weeks the Olympic Games are starting in Vancouver. My Olympic Games. I've missed them not once, but twice—in 2002 and 2006. I'm twenty-nine years old, and this might just be my only shot at Olympic glory. In Vancouver, in the 1500 meters, it's got to happen. Everything I've done until this point must come together.

In the two weeks leading up to this all-important race, all kinds of questions run through my head. What if I fail miserably? What if I've been training all these years for nothing? What if for the rest of my life I'll be forced to look back on this day with regret?

You might recognize these kinds of questions if you put a lot of time, energy, and love into your work, your relationship, or something else in your life you find meaningful. These are questions that inevitably arise when taking on a challenge, though when you need to perform, they don't exactly help.

In those tense weeks before the 2010 Olympic Games, I read about Stoic philosophy for the first time. Whether I have it to thank for my gold medal, I cannot say. But since then I haven't stopped reading about and applying Stoic ideas. Developing a Stoic mindset has made me both more relaxed and more driven.

We are accustomed—and this definitely goes for professional athletes—to the idea that we can control our world and force certain results. At the same time, we also understand that we don't truly have that power: opponents can be better, the market can be up or down, a pandemic can suddenly throw a wrench in the works, or you can just have plain bad luck. The real world is chaotic, hard, and unpredictable. How can we train ourselves to better handle this? To stay true to ourselves, to find peace and fulfillment while chasing our dreams?

I found the answer to these questions in Stoicism, a school of thought that emerged in ancient Greece around 300 BC and is

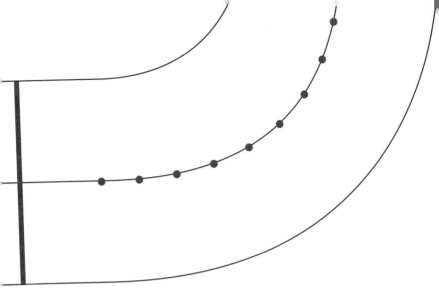

characterized by practical wisdom. Stoicism resonated with the Romans for centuries as well. It's especially from this Roman period that a number of important texts have fortunately survived, and I devoured these works in particular. From **Seneca**: a learned, ambitious orator, writer, and statesman. From **Marcus Aurelius**: a wise, dutiful emperor. And from **Epictetus**: a man, born into slavery, who was given freedom and revealed himself to be a stern yet celebrated teacher.

The Stoic mindset helped me channel my drive and continues to make me calmer, more effective, and more successful. Not just during my speed skating career, but also after I stopped: when I needed to enter the job market despite knowing little more than how to skate laps, when I took my first steps as an entrepreneur, and when I became a father and all of a sudden that became more important to me than the rest.

What appeals to me most is that the main Stoics were anything but idle, daydreaming philosophers. They were engaged with the world around them, took a stand, and looked for ways, in spite of everything, to lead the best life possible. In chapter 8, I'll address what "the best life possible" means but for now it's enough to understand that Stoic philosophy focuses on a power hidden within every person. The external factors are not what's important—it's that you get the best out of yourself and do good by others.

That's why Stoicism remains so popular today. Compared to a thousand years ago, the world has changed drastically, but Stoicism touches on natural values—on a way of thinking that's still deeply rooted in us as human beings.

I believe life becomes more fun and interesting through learning, searching, and taking risks—in short: tapping into your own "drive." At the same time, I also believe that life becomes nicer and more beautiful through experiencing calm, peace, and fulfillment. One side doesn't have to exclude the other; indeed, for me they complement each other. From a place of peace and calm you're able to learn better, live better, and know when to take risks. By developing and training a Stoic mindset, you can lead your life focused and relaxed, whether you're a professional athlete, fireman, soldier, lawyer, bricklayer, teacher, or king.

This book was written to share with you my interpretation and implementation of the Stoics' lessons. I have distilled all the Stoic texts, exercises, and applications I've encountered into ten principles. They've served me as a guide to cultivating a Stoic mindset. In this book I'll show you how I employ these principles in my own life—at one time as a professional athlete, now as an entrepreneur and as a father.

But *The Stoic Mindset* isn't a handbook telling you exactly what you need to do. I encourage you above all to go out and seek the Stoic mindset that fits you. At the end of each chapter you'll find an exercise to help you master the Stoic mindset. These exercise have been designed in collaboration with a sport psychologist, and I still use them daily. See this book as an initiation into Stoic thought and action. I believe that if you know how to apply these ten principles, you will learn to make more valuable choices and better steer yourself.

USE
SETBACKS

AS SIGNPOSTS

The impediment to action advances action. What stands in the way becomes the way.

~ *Marcus Aurelius*

Conquering the world, proving I'm the best—that's what my life is about as a twenty-one-year-old speed skater. It's 2001, and I'm working toward next year's Olympic Games. I'm going to win everything over the coming year, and I write my future triumphs on the calendar. Failure doesn't exist for me. I am the youngest and most promising speed skater in the Netherlands.

In order to cash in on my career plans, I lay it on thick while negotiating my contract with my sponsor. They love the ambition I radiate and are taken with my story. I land a big deal, obviously with the caveat that certain achievements are expected of me. Welcome to the hard and results-oriented world of professional sports.

To make good on that promise, I scrap all rest days from my training schedule. At practice I do more than is asked of me. If we have to skate ten laps, I do eleven. If we go to a training camp for three weeks, I stay an extra three days, and if I have to bike for two hours, I always make it three. Working harder means skating harder, right?

That's what I tell myself in any case, but I'm overdoing things in my eagerness to perform. I'm personally not all that aware of it—I've got blinders on—until my body grinds to a halt. I get sick and tired at the weirdest moments. As soon as I recover, I jack up my training schedule to make up for lost time, which only leads me to get sick again.

I'm walking to a training camp in Inzell, Germany, when things take a turn for the worse. It's freezing cold, dark, and I'm tired before even setting foot on the ice. I fight with the voice in my head that says, "This is pointless. Why don't you just turn around? Why don't you go home?" I ignore that voice, put on my skates, and after a couple of laps conclude that I'm exhausted and things can't go on like this.

Just three months before the Olympic Games kick off in Salt Lake City, Utah, there's something seriously wrong with me. I'm sick and seriously overtrained, a lot like burnout in normal life. In 2002, the Netherlands wins eight Olympic medals, but I'm not there. On the couch at home, I can barely muster the courage to turn on the TV. Although it pains me, I watch how the medals are divided.

So, there I am, lying like a patient in bed. Of course I can hear the commentators in the speed skating world: it's the end of the road for Tuitert. It drives me crazy for not being too far from the truth. As a young talent, you've only got a few years to make your breakthrough. If by your early twenties, you still haven't shown what you're capable of, you can forget about a great career. My dream is falling apart because I worked too hard for it. A nightmare.

A philosophy born out of adversity

If only I'd known then about Stoicism, a school of philosophy that never would have existed without adversity. It would take years before I came into contact with the Stoics, though I could have really benefitted from them back in 2002. From works, for example, by Zeno of Citium (335–262 BC), a wealthy Phoenician merchant and the founder of Stoicism. Shipwrecked near Athens around the year 300 BC, he was forced to give up his precious cargo: he lost nearly all his possessions at one fell swoop.

THE STOIC FREELANCER

The freedom of being my own boss appealed to me: I've done a lot of jobs while self-employed. The more you work, the more your earn—it gave me a good feeling. But this can also turn into a trap. You need to learn how to say no to jobs that don't reward you enough or don't fit with what it is you want to do.

Visualizing undesirable situations (Practicing Setbacks), found at the end of this chapter, can help you with this. You can imagine a negotiation floundering, or calling off a job because it pays too little. Would the world crumble if that happened? No, probably not. A Stoic entrepreneur will know the value of their work, and will dare to say no every now and then.

He wound up on the Agora, the marketplace in ancient Athens—at the time not only the spot where business was conducted but also the beating heart of education, philosophy, and debate. His shipwreck became reason to give his life a new direction and to dedicate himself to philosophy.

Step one for Zeno was to get to know the works of famous philosophers. He studied under the philosopher Crates. Zeno would draw many ideas from Crates, who belonged to the school of Cynic philosophers—ideas such as gender equality, which back then was a radical view. But above all, Zeno was inspired by the practical philosophy of Socrates (469–399 BC). In the end, he set up his own philosophical school in the painted porch beside the Agora, the Stoa Poikile. He'd lost everything and went searching for what was possible. He strove toward, in his own words, "practicing philosophy with less baggage." "Now that I've suffered shipwreck," he said, "I'm on a good journey." In other words: adversity is the source of Stoic philosophy.

Unlike his great inspiration Socrates, who was condemned to drinking hemlock, Zeno was honored as a highly respected citizen of Athens. He was seen as a man valuable in every way, in particular for teaching young people and so bringing out the best in others. After his death, Zeno's

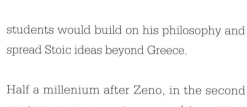

students would build on his philosophy and spread Stoic ideas beyond Greece.

Half a millenium after Zeno, in the second century AD, we meet a second important Stoic philosopher, the Roman emperor Marcus Aurelius (121–180 AD). To cope with the challenges facing an emperor at that time— fighting corruption, leading his army against Germanic tribes—he trained himself in Stoicism with the help of philosophy teachers.

This philosophy aided him in state affairs, but it also taught him how to cope with setbacks: his wife and nine of his fourteen children would die during his lifetime, and if that wasn't enough, he was betrayed by his most valued general. With that much adversity, you could use some Stoic philosophy.

Marcus Aurelius gave his own spin to Zeno's philosophy: he told himself that everything in life, even adversity, was useful. He drew a comparison with a fire to illustrate this point. A small fire dies out at the first setback; throw something onto it, and it goes out. However, if the fire is big enough, it will devour everything you might throw onto it. In fact, it blazes even higher. What was once adversity becomes fuel.

Marcus Aurelius used the setbacks he was

faced with as fuel for his own fire. In one of his texts, notes originally intended as reminders for himself rather than for others, he wrote: "This is not bad luck, but rather it is my good luck that, although this has happened to me, I can bear it without pain, neither crushed by the present nor fearful of the future." A fine example of a Stoic mindset.

You can learn to handle adversity

Stoic philosophy emerged in a time of great hardship. Society was regularly ravaged by devastating wars, famines, and epidemics. It was therefore important to arm yourself both physically and mentally. Nowadays, certainly in the West, we're more likely to die from overabundance than scarcity, and that brings with it different challenges. Setbacks are rarer and we mainly have to teach ourselves how to deal with excess: excess of news, information via our telephones, food—the list goes on. Should we want to live a good life, it's wise to arm ourselves against excess instead.

Sometimes we rediscover old rituals to do so. When it comes to fasting or taking ice baths, you might think of modern influencers trying to sell us healthy lifestyles from their mansions on Ibiza, but these methods are as old as the road to Rome. Seneca (4 BC–65 AD), another Roman Stoic, used to douse himself in ice water. Though good for his body, it was mainly to train himself to deal with hardships.

When you're lying safely in bed, you're probably not worrying about hunger or the freezing cold, but by thinking about what you *are* scared of you can better deal with adversity. What if you lost your job tomorrow? What if everyone laughed at you during that crucial presentation? With it already in mind, you don't have to be shaken up if it actually happens to you.

Too often, we expect that our lives will follow some predictable, manicured path. Everything might be cruising along nicely, exactly as planned, until—BAM!—things take a very different turn. What do you do then? What if your partner ends your relationship? If you're fired? Or a pandemic breaks out, just to name a few?

Everyone with a bit of life experience knows these kinds of things can happen. Setbacks are part of life. On the one hand, you can have a passionate dream, the happy expectation of what you plan to achieve in life, and on the other hand the pain that arises when something fails.

You can rub salt in the wound by blaming yourself when things don't succeed, but this only traps you in the past. You can also look to the future and learn from your mistakes. A Stoic would say it's fine to enjoy the expectation of a dream as long as you can rid yourself of the negative feelings that arise if that dream doesn't pan out, which is a real possibility. Guaranteed success doesn't exist, having to deal with setbacks, however, is a fact of life.

Plenty of careers have blossomed only after overcoming setbacks. Adversity forces you to take a step back or adapt. Adversity humbles. Adversity challenges. And it forces you to readjust.

One of the most important laws of training is that of adaptation: training our bodies is nothing more than damaging it slightly so that our muscles are forced to not just recover but grow even stronger to better withstand the next stimulus. In evolution it's not the law of the strongest that counts; it's the survival of the best-adapted. We are made to create something new from rubble, something better.

Writer and philosopher Nassim Nicholas Taleb, inspired, among others, by the Stoics, uses a nice term for things that gain strength from setbacks: "anti-fragile." This is the opposite of fragile and means they benefit from damage, on the condition that the damage doesn't kill them. Those who can convert damage into growth don't just survive, they grow thanks to setbacks.

Salt Lake City, 2002

While my teammates are dazzling at the Olympic Games and others speculating about the end of my speed skating career, I try to make sense of what happened to me. My curious nature comes in handy: I dive into books and educate myself about training theory, psychology, and philosophy. I take notes in my notebook day after day.

Although I won't discover Stoic philosophy until later, I find out there are many athletes who've made the same mistakes as I have. And not just athletes: in every field and every situation many people put on blinders, because of which they fail to recognize warning signs and eventually hit a wall. I read biographies of athletes who had to go through deep lows before winning competitions, as well as entrepreneurs who fell flat before scrambling back up. It gives me hope and inspiration to keep going. There's no nicely paved highway to the top.

Thankfully, I make a recovery after the winter of 2002. One morning, I go for a run through a forest and track my heart rate, as it needs to stay below 130 beats per minute (bpm). I'm forced to face reality when I'm overtaken by my neighbor, thirty years my senior. I know I need to keep a low profile so as not to fall into the same trap—that I must stick to my assignment. My salvation is that I know what happened to me, through what I've learned about it. It prepares me for my future.

The art of living is more like wrestling than dancing, insofar as it stands ready against the accidental and the unforeseen, and is not apt to fall.
~ Marcus Aurelius

I don't have much use for speed skating exercises now that I've stopped being a professional athlete, but what I read on the couch in those days, what I learned about my body and mind, I still apply every day.

For example, I learned to picture potential setbacks in detail, in order to find the calm and the strength to never be shaken up, no matter how lousy the situation. I also learned that I have the adaptive capability to grow both physically and mentally through adversity and so am no longer scared of it. For that I can thank missing the Olympic Games, perhaps the biggest setback I could imagine at the time.

Don't get me wrong—I still get bummed out by setbacks, and if I had the choice, I'd do without them. But if you want to raise the bar, want to learn things, you need to take risks. There's no other way. And if you take risks and chase your dreams, there will inevitably come a time when things don't go your way. No matter how bad a setback can feel at such a moment, it's all part of a rich and challenging life. A setback is a signpost, not a stop sign.

EXERCISE 1
PRACTICING SETBACKS

In order to be able to accept adversity, the Stoics tried to picture setbacks as clearly as possible. This allows you to train your thoughts about them, just like muscles.

STEP 1 Think of a situation that you're worried about—for example, a contract renewal.

STEP 2 Now imagine the most undesirable outcome: your contract isn't renewed.

STEP 3 Grab a piece of paper and draw a circle. Make it nice and big so you can write a lot inside of it.

STEP 4 Now in the circle write at least ten words or phrases that you associate with this most undesirable outcome. Money worries, losing your home, etc.

STEP 5 Give this outcome a title or name and write it above the circle: "If I lose my job."

STEP 6 Now, outside of the circle, write a few keywords and ideas about how you can deal with this outcome. Saving more, learning new skills, asking friends for support, etc.

When you've done this exercise, your fear of this undesirable situation diminishes because now you're prepared.

LESSON 2

JUDGE LESS,

**UNDERSTAND
MORE**

It is not things in themselves that trouble us, but our judgments of them.

~ *Epictetus*

As a child, you don't expect your parents to divorce. After all, parents understand how the world works and know what they're doing, right? They might sometimes fight, sure, but divorce? Never.

Just as I'm making my breakthrough in speed skating, around 1999, it happens anyway. Sadness, love, incomprehension, and pain translate themselves into a crazy cocktail of emotions between my mom and dad. I butt heads, in particular, with my dad over this. I can see he's angry and at a loss with a situation that has degenerated into divorce. But I don't really understand his anger and even find myself getting angry at him in turn. He's an adult, isn't he?

I take my mom's side. I help her by buying her a house and trying to support her. I don't do much with the anger I feel at my dad—I distance myself from him. I don't attempt to understand the situation on a deeper level, and instead I try to focus entirely on skating. My judgment is fixed: he's in the wrong, he's the bad guy, and so I break all contact. He only creates negative energy anyway.

"He's still your dad," I hear people saying, but I shrug them off. It's a severe decision, but at that moment it feels like the only right one. I don't want to be the plaything of emotions that constantly get out of hand.

Room for emotions

It's a big misconception that Stoics strive toward ignoring their emotions, in the same way the word "stoic" is often used in our everyday language. Emotions are part of human nature, they're in our DNA, we can't switch them off. As children, we learn to recognize emotions, usually from our parents, but also from other people in our surroundings. That connects us with others.

According to the Stoics, emotions are the result of our judgments about events. An emotion is fundamentally neither good nor bad. It's a reflection of your judgment and your thoughts about a situation.

The Stoics try not to act on immediate emotion. In other words: they endeavor to not make choices based on frustration, rage, and euphoria. Instead, they try to understand the thinking and judgments behind their emotions so as to make better decisions.

How can you better understand those emotions? Simple: by thinking them over and asking yourself the right questions. We are capable of having emotions and at the same time reflecting on them: "I'm furious, that's a fact, but why is that?" That's one of our great attributes as human beings.

Seneca uses the metaphor of a wound as illustration. You can suffer a physical wound in an accident, but if you treat it properly, after a while you won't be troubled by it anymore. However, if a good friend offends you deeply, that inflicts another kind of wound. A deep emotional scar. Whereas we naturally analyze how to heal physical wounds, we often let mental wounds fester. That's a shame because they can trouble you for the rest of your life.

The Stoics tried to treat emotional pain just like physical pain. They sought to expose the judgments *behind* pain in order to heal it. It's not for nothing that ancient philosophers were seen as doctors of the soul, comparable to psychologists or psychiatrists today. And it's not for nothing that we see Stoic philosophy used in modern cognitive behavioral therapy.

How can you understand an emotion? An emotion just happens to you, doesn't it? Maybe it's good to make a distinction between your first impression and the emotion that follows it. The first immediate impression that we feel—we have no influence over this. The immediate pain after a fall or the adrenaline that screams through your body when a car slams on the brakes in front of you are examples of a first impression.

An old Stoic tale that exemplifies the difference between emotion and first impression tells of a prominent Stoic teacher. He's sitting with the other passengers on a ship caught in a heavy storm. The waves are huge, and the ship threatens to overturn. The Stoic goes pale like everyone else and looks just as terrified as the other passengers. But the Stoic keeps his calm, unlike the others, who scream and lament the end of the world. When the wind dies back down and the waves calm, one of the passengers goes to the Stoic and asks him why his face had been pale like all the rest. "That's not exactly Stoic, is it?," they say. The Stoic answers that even a wise person still feels first impressions, but they don't convert those impressions into emotions. A wise person can be unnerved for a moment, and then gathers themself quickly.

By applying a Stoic mindset, you learn to feel fear, just like everybody else, while choosing not to go along with that first impression. You don't suppress this fear, but you take control of it by not reacting to that first impression with your thoughts. The result is that you can stay calm and act accordingly.

Take a soccer player who has lost a game and says with anger and disappointment that they "deserved to win." That's a nice example of what Epictetus (50–135 AD), a Stoic born into slavery, described as "emotions resulting from a wrong judgment," namely that this soccer player has the right to win. The player judges the outcome as unfair and is now expressing his anger in front of the cameras. However, if he lingers in that anger, he won't be as quick to think about what he could do next time to improve his chances of winning.

Another example: if an entrepreneur is jealous of a competitor with better sales, this conceals a personal judgment that their own product is just as good, or perhaps even better than the competition. By only busying themself with their jealousy, the entrepreneur is focused on the other and not on their own product, service, or marketing. This makes their chances of being more successful even lower.

Victimhood of this kind was nothing new for Epictetus, who taught that no one but ourself is responsible for our own judgments. This lesson from Epictetus also applies when someone tries to throw you off balance by provoking you. You can choose not to respond, not to act based on your first emotional reaction. Should you react, then you become an accomplice in the provocation because it was your own choice to do so.

Not acting on your first impression does not mean you shouldn't act at all. Seneca chose to pursue the bandits who robbed and killed his father. He didn't, however, do this out of rage, but rather love for his father and to make sure the bandits wouldn't be able to claim more victims. He thought over his first impression and then acted calmly and judiciously.

One of the basic principles of a Stoic mindset is that you consider your emotions. You can worry about the future, but a Stoic will ask themself: Why? Why are you scared of losing your job? Why are you jealous? What is the judgment underlying that emotion? Might you be angry because, in your view, someone did a great injustice to you? And what is this feeling of injustice based on?

This allows you to examine your own judgment, cultivate a better

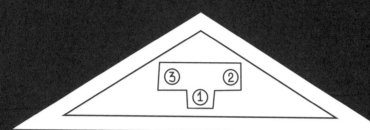

THE STOIC ATHLETE

No matter at what level you compete, you perform the best and enjoy a sport the most when losing yourself in the physical activity, in the moment. What you shouldn't do, above all, is worry about the outcome of others, because you have no influence over them.

The fastest way to lose your concentration and focus is to let yourself be provoked. Whether you're behind in an Olympic final or on the soccer field, it's your choice to be distracted by others. Lose your concentration, and you'll lose your enjoyment, your result. Focus on the task and the physical feeling of doing the sport that makes you happy.

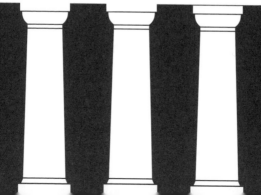

understanding of your own emotions, and be able to better empathize with others, whether that's your parents, colleagues, friends, loved ones, or strangers. You'll be able to free yourself from your own negative judgments, to oversee situations calmly, and, from a place of peace, decide the best way to react. Now, that's real positive thinking.

Questioning your own judgments

Five years after breaking contact with my father, I realize that although I've learned a lot in speed skating, my challenges lie elsewhere. If I want to become a better skater, I first have to become a better person.

I have an amazing team and one of the best trainers in the world—Jac Orie—but something is still off. A piece of the puzzle is missing. At twenty-five years old, in the prime of my life, I should be at the top of my game every week and yet I haven't placed for an individual event at the 2006 Games in Turin. I figure out that what's behind my disappointing performances doesn't have anything to do with my skating, my profession, but everything to do with my judgments and my choices, which are affecting other parts of my life. I resolve to call my dad.

It took some time. I didn't dare to do it right away, because I was afraid of his reaction; that he would be angry or instead sad. But I also knew that if I didn't call, nothing would change for either of us. How often does it happen that people only realize on their deathbeds that they should've dropped fights sooner? That would be a shame. And I understood this situation was costing a lot of energy now too.

I waited until I was far away from home before calling him. I'd just had a training session in preparation for a World Cup. I was standing next to the ice rink when I called him.

My dad's reaction was not the one I'd feared for so long. Rather, he was happy I'd reached out to him: time heals some wounds, or at least ensures a thin scab.

Real freedom was much closer than I could have imagined. For me, the last puzzle piece was not the right trainer or a perfect training program. Real freedom lay in the last place I dared look: myself—or rather, my judgments, like my judgment about my father.

My judgment had never progressed beyond that first impression, that first emotional reaction of anger. As long as my behavior was purely based on that first emotion, based on that first judgment, I could only stay angry. I wasn't free to decide how I dealt with the situation.

That all is as thinking makes it so—and you control your thinking. So remove your judgments whenever you wish and then there is calm—as the sailor rounding the cape finds smooth water and the welcome of a waveless bay.

~ Marcus Aurelius

After this conversation with my dad, I realized where my anger was coming from. It was linked to my opinion about what it means to be a dad and what I craved from my dad: unconditional love, support, and understanding. I felt a lot of injustice over the situation, while I had no idea what it meant to be a father and didn't want to take the trouble to understand his feelings of powerlessness. Another nice example of Epictetus's belief that emotions based on wrong judgments are harmful. I only clung more dearly to my own conviction. It was when I was honest about the judgment behind my emotion, by saying to myself that I honestly didn't know what it meant to be a father, that I recognized his powerlessness and saw what my dad had done for me.

From that moment on, I was able to focus all my energy on my goal, on my own struggle. And that had nothing to do with my parents—and actually nothing to do with winning Olympic gold either. My struggle has to do with giving absolutely everything at the right moment.

I know I've got a lot more in me than I've shown, but until then I've rarely succeeded in demonstrating that on the ice. I feel more energy and peace now that I've jettisoned my previous judgment. A weight has slipped from my shoulders. And not just my own shoulders: four years later, during my Olympic race in Vancouver, my father shows up and from the stands, finally, cheers for me.

EXERCISE 2
THE ABCs OF EMOTION

This exercise will help you see that an emotion (C) that you're
feeling doesn't immediately follow from an event (A) but from
your judgment about this event (B). You can question, explore,
and change this thought at B.

STEP 1 Grab a piece of paper and write A B C underneath each other.

STEP 2 Think of a situation that made you very angry, frustrated, tense,
sad, or disappointed. Describe, as objectively as possible, what the
situation was or is at A.

⟶ I'm failing to manage a project on my own.

STEP 3 Then at C write as carefully as possible how you felt.

⟶ Frustrated, since no one is helping me.

STEP 4 At B write the thought, opinion, conviction, or judgment
causing you to feel as you've described at C.

⟶ Asking for help is a form of weakness.

STEP 5 Now cross out your answer at B. What can you write instead
that will change the outcome at C? *Asking for help is an option for
solving this.* At C this could then change into: *I feel relief because
a colleague is now helping me.*

With this exercise you can learn how to change the
useless and negatively charged thought at B into a
positively charged one. And as a result,
your emotion will also change.

LESSON
3

All things can be divided into two categories: that which does lie within the boundaries of our control and that which does not.

~ Epictetus

Everybody wants to do well, to succeed, to win. Winning feels great and is addictive. It won't come as a surprise that in my years as a professional athlete I was obsessed with it. But if you're so crazy about winning, professional sports is really not your best option.

A simple calculation will teach you that the chances of disappointment are much higher than those of success. You actually have to be a little nuts to think you'll be the one to win everything, despite the athletes who participate in the Games already being a selection of the best from their countries. And out of all those top athletes, only one can win.

It wasn't until I was twenty-nine, nearly retirement age for a professional athlete, that I finally got my shot at the ultimate win.

As I walk into the Olympic speed skating stadium in Vancouver, the stands fill with Dutch supporters. The royal family is sitting in the place of honor, and there are cameras everywhere. The world is watching.

I can see the tense look in my competitors' eyes and of course feel the nerves too: these are the Olympic Games, unlike any other competition. I trained twelve years for this moment, for the less than two minutes in which everything must come together. I missed the Olympic 1500 meters twice in a row: in 2002, I lay exhausted at home on my couch, and in 2006, a major gaffe during the Olympic qualifiers cost me a ticket to the Games in Turin. Today, February 20, 2010, is the first and probably last chance I will get in my life to secure Olympic gold.

Such a deeply cherished desire can change into fear just before a race like this, with the understanding that wishes don't always come true. All kinds of things can go wrong: I can be unlucky with my opponent during the crossover; my great rival, Shani Davis, from the USA can have the race of his life; the starter can wait too long with the starting shot; the ice can be just a little worse during my race. All of it can influence the result, and this can drive you crazy.

In the weeks before the race, all of these questions flashed through my mind: What if I fall? Or come in 30th? Or, much worse, fourth? Was it all worth it then? The sacrifice, the disappointment?

These are understandable thoughts. Ask a performer how they feel just before going onstage, ask a soldier about to head into a battle, ask a politician who has to make a speech—everyone knows the fear that comes before something important. Something toward which they've been working for so long and don't want to go wrong. This fear is a natural emotion, though right before you intend to perform, it can really get in the way. That's why I try to reign in my thoughts. However, that's easier said than done.

Control only what you can control

One of the foremost principles of a Stoic mindset is that you can divide things into that which you can control and that which you can't. In that regard, the Stoics keep things simple. Epictetus, a Greek Stoic, knew what he was talking about: he was born into slavery and experienced firsthand that he didn't have control over many situations that we, being free, take for granted. He managed to stay calm even when, on one occasion, his master exploded in rage and broke Epictetus's leg.

Protesting or getting angry was pointless. In fact, by getting angry he would only be handing his master more power. Epictetus chose not to grant him that power; he controlled his own reaction, in that way maintaining power over himself.

This was the only thing he could control—not what his master did. As a true Stoic, he'd trained himself to endure physical pain, such as that of breaking a bone, and maintaining control over his own mood, independent of any pain.

Epictetus gained his freedom as a young man and founded his own philosophy school. He must have been a strict teacher. Epictetus regularly accused his followers of being "slaves" or "wretches" when they let themselves get too carried away by first impressions. "Stay strong, slave, don't get swept away!" he would shout.

A former enslaved person constantly accusing others of being slaves—if there was anyone who could do it, it was Epictetus, and he didn't pass up the opportunity. He consciously employed this tactic against people who complained without realizing it. And he had a strong point: those who let their actions be determined by circumstances they couldn't control, allowed themselves to be enslaved by those circumstances. That's why Epictetus found the divide between what you could and couldn't control paramount. Wealth, health, and victory are, according to this view, outside your control. I didn't understand that right away. Don't I do my best to live healthily, to earn money, and to win a race? That's within my power—I choose to do it, don't I?

Exactly! You can indeed do your utmost best, and leave no stone unturned, but the result of "doing your best" is not up to you. The only things you can influence are the way you play, the way you work, the way you apply yourself: those are on you.

The Stoic analogy of an archer wanting to hit their mark fits nicely here. The only thing the archer can ensure is that they shoot as straight and as accurately as possible. They can tune their bow perfectly and learn how to control their breathing, but as soon as that arrow is let go, what happens next is no longer up to them. The arrows seeks the mark. The ultimate goal of the archer is to prepare themselves as best as possible, to carry out every task for shooting as best as possible. It's the same with our lives. It's not about hitting the bull's-eye—it's about becoming the greatest archers we can be.

Even a good sharpshooter can miss. An archer possessed by the goal knows neither peace nor resignation. But the archer who let's go of the target finds peace in the execution—and that's exactly the kind of Stoic calm that can enrich your life.

THE STOIC ENTREPRENEUR

Being an entrepreneur is intense. Every decision starts and ends with you, and often there's no playbook to fall back on. In my company, we produce chewing gum. In 2020, our packaging factory partially burned down because of riots. In one stroke, our revenue stream dried up because we no longer had a product.

The only thing you can do as an entrepreneur is focus on what you can control. So, we used the time to focus everything on the launch of our new website. On a personal level, it was the time in which I lay the foundation for this book. Focusing on what you can actually do, on new chances—that's energizing.

*　*　*

Companies, politicians, and coaches try to convince us that results are entirely up to us, and this gives us the sense that we can control every outcome in our lives. But when you go deeper, you discover this isn't the case. A lot of what happens to us is sheer luck. We plainly do not have the power to control everything. We can get sick, we can go bust, we can lose—those things happen, but does that immediately mean failure? Such an attitude can weigh on you, and gets in the way of your life satisfaction and a good result. There's no need for that.

For a practiced Stoic, their health, body, living situation, whether they are rich or poor, fail or succeed, ultimately have no influence on their peace of mind. With a Stoic mindset, you separate happiness and mood from external circumstances or goals. Experiencing happiness is completely independent of your own interpretation and effort.

That's why Stoics focus all their energy on making the right choices, because unlike outcomes, you have full control over your decisions. Frustrations about not achieving goals, bad luck, or chance—they get set aside. Stoics make the radical choice to not waste energy on what's not in their hands.

When you apply this Stoic mindset, your life becomes more manageable and focused. At the end of this chapter I'll show you how to make a plan for those things you can influence and how to implement it. You set aside what's outside your control, creating clarity and peace. By thinking in this way, your chances of achieving the goal in mind actually increase. You win by not focusing on winning.

The golden race

As I step onto the ice and look at the packed stands, I can hear the spectators' excitement. It's Saturday night, and the highlight of the speed skating competition is about to begin.

In the changing rooms below the stands, I focus on what I've learned from Epictetus and Seneca. What my competitors do, what others think of me, whether the ice is good or bad—all of that is beyond my control. I push the thought of winning gold from my mind.

What I can do something about, in that last moment before the gun goes off, is have courage. However, being courageous doesn't mean no longer experiencing fear. Courage is feeling fear and still taking action. Courage is the best counterbalance against fear in every situation.

I can feel the fear of having trained for nothing, the fear of failing again, the fear of letting my only chance at gold slip through my fingers.

I intentionally shrink my world in my head and let other thoughts fade away. I've trained against losing myself in first impressions, not falling into the slavery that Epictetus warned us of.

All my attention goes to the first few strides I have to hit when the gun goes off. If I want a chance at winning, everything needs to be right from the start. I have influence over that—the rest is noise. This is now my entire world. If I lose, then I'll do it with my head held high. Win or lose, no regrets, no complaints or excuses.

A more powerful idea doesn't exist in my mind. I can perform to the best of my ability and keep calm by not worrying about winning gold. And as I'm calm, I'm also precise. One minute, forty-five seconds and fifty-seven milliseconds later, I win gold.

Who then is invincible? The one who cannot be upset by anything outside their reasoned choice.

~ Epictetus

EXERCISE 3
BULL'S-EYE

With the following technique, you can order your thoughts to be able to distinguish between what you have control over and what you don't.

STEP 1 Grab a sheet of paper and draw a big circle. Then draw a smaller circle inside it, like the red center of a dartboard. Make them both nice and big; you'll need to be able to write plenty inside them.

STEP 2 Think of a goal you want to achieve. It can be anything: from giving a stellar presentation to spending more time with your kids.

STEP 3 Write in the outermost circle everything outside your control. Don't forget to name all the obvious things, like the weather. Be sure to include the one you really can't do anything about: the result.

STEP 4 Now in the innermost circle, mention everything that you do have influence over. According to the Stoics, those are, strictly speaking, just your own choices and actions, but this can differ for your situation.

If you're overthinking how to deal with the problem, turn first to the bull's-eye. What lies in the innermost circle? Make a plan for that. And in the outermost? Set all that aside.

WHAT'S GOOD

GOOD FOR YOU FOR THE TEAM IS

What is not good for
the swarm is not good
for the bee.

~ *Marcus Aurelius*

At the beginning of my speed skating career I'm a true all-rounder—not a specialist, but pretty good at everything. I train with the sprinters and the distance skaters.

I train with Gianni Romme and Erben Wennemars, accomplished athletes in my sport, and at practice we're always trying to one up each other. We aren't just teammates, we're also competitors for the same medals. That goes for the sport as well as working life. We have our sights on the same jobs, the same clients, or the same budgets, though without cooperation we won't be achieving any of it.

There's a reason speed skaters skate in a single-file line. By blocking the wind, you help one another reach a higher level. But there's a trap: when individual egos start to outweigh team interest, the willingness to help one another falls by the wayside. The sprinter might skate so fast that no one can keep up with them, or the long-distance skater might take lap after lap at a brutal pace, forcing the others to drop off. Each of them can give themself a pat on the back and nod with satisfaction, thinking, "I was the best today."

The result, however, is that within no time everybody will be skating on their own. No one will block the wind for anyone else anymore. One skater's drive to perform comes at the expense of another skater— and ultimately everyone's level drops. Their egos might get stroked, but the overall performance suffers—and the enjoyment is gone.

A good understanding of yourself and others

Given that someone with a Stoic mindset focuses on personal development and their character, you might think that Stoicism is geared toward the individual. And you're right that for the Stoics it's all about

THE STOIC PARENT

Children are flawless at finding your weak spots (and those of their brothers and sisters). How can you stay Stoic as a parent? Seneca would say, "Count to ten" (this trick is attributed to him), though that's often easier said than done.

My wife and I are trying to impart to our children a dash of Stoic self-reflection. When our daughter shouts: "My little brother is stupid," we try to explain to her that this isn't true and that what she actually means is "I think my little brother is behaving stupidly." In that way she says that she only finds her brother's *behavior* annoying, not him as a person.

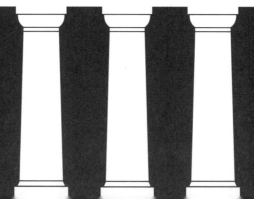

having a good rapport with yourself; however, it's equally important to have a good rapport with others.

Self-preservation is our first natural impulse, the Stoics say, and this isn't far-fetched if you look at nature: we are a product of the survival strategies of our ancestors. But Stoicism doesn't stop at self-preservation.

That self-preservation strategy leads to social behavior. Doing good by others is a survival strategy for social creatures. In that sense, you can't do anything good for yourself when it's at the expense of another. Here I mean "good" in the Stoic sense of the word, which has nothing to do with external factors such as a good outcome. (After all, you can't do anything about that, as we saw in the previous chapter.)

One of the aspects of Stoic "good" is the endeavor to treat everyone in the world just as well as you treat yourself and the people close to you, regardless of their background, status, race or personality. According to Seneca, it is our duty to mean something to others, preferably a lot. And if that's not possible, then to a small group, to the people close to you, and if all else fails then you still need to mean something to yourself.

The most important successor to Zeno, the founder of Stoicism, was Chrysippus of Soli, who lived in the third century BC. He was, besides a philosopher, a passionate runner, and also studied under Cleanthes, a passionate boxer. See that? Sports and philosophy make an outstanding combination.

Chrysippus was rather fanatic in his work as a philosopher: throughout his life he wrote more than 700 works. He was a brilliant thinker and expert in argumentation, with which he lay a sturdy logical foundation beneath Stoic philosophy. He was also one of the first with the ambition and self-confidence to spread Stoic thought beyond the traditional gates of the Agora in Athens. Without Chrysippus we wouldn't know of Stoic philosophy today.

According to Chrysippus, a runner should do their utmost to win a race, though never by tripping another. And it's the same in life: it's good to strive for something, as long you don't do it at the expense of another.

Winning or losing are in themselves neither good nor bad. For a Stoic, the term "good" is all about justice. Doing good by yourself and by others are interconnected. Your family, your friends, your neighborhood, your town, your country, the world, yourself: we are all connected by the same human nature.

When you do something that's bad for the community, then it's also bad for you. You can cheat in Monopoly or as a professional athlete resort to doping to clinch victory, but with time no one will want to play with you, or you'll be suspended for cheating. The fun of the game is gone—not just for others but for you.

Stoics, with Chrysippus at the fore, didn't retreat into their own bubbles. They were people of the world. They were politicians and asked them-

selves how they could contribute to the greater good. The mental freedom they strove for was part of doing well by others and meaning something to them. Absolute autonomy doesn't exist in this sense according to the Stoics: we are all connected with one another and work together to achieve goals—that's ingrained in our nature. Plus: What are experiences worth if you can't share them with others?

To drive this point home, Stoics often compare our behavior with our bodies. According to the Roman emperor Marcus Aurelius, the limbs of our bodies are comparable to the people in a community: they are made to work together. You don't develop real strength by pumping up one muscle, but instead by making multiple muscles work together. In the same way, you don't solve a complex problem by locking yourself in your attic, but by working together with others and brainstorming possible solutions.

TOGETHER
126,000,000 seconds

ALONE
105 seconds

Neighborliness

You can find a nice example of this in the eastern Netherlands, where I grew up on a farm. There, we have a well-known concept called *noaberschap*, or neighborliness, and it's the unwritten rule that neighbors are duty-bound to help one another. If a farmer gets sick, their neighbors take over the work on their property. The pact is mutual. Neighborliness originated as a kind of health insurance in remote areas, where the community dealt with unexpected individual blows by sharing the resulting burden and working together. You could say this is the basis of our social democracy: it is our duty to help another in need. And in that way this unwritten rule forms the glue of our community. Self-preservation and community spirit aren't a contradiction, they go hand in hand.

In professional sports it's all about details. A hair's breadth can mean the difference between winning and losing at the finish line. But the real difference is made long before then.

My Olympic 1500 meters lasted one minute, forty-five seconds, and fifty-seven milliseconds, a little over a hundred and five seconds. The four-year run-up to the Olympic Games consists of 126 million seconds. That means that the final stretch, the part I have to do on my own, is 0.00000083 percent of the whole. To be able to perform at my very best in that final stretch, I need to be improving a little each day until then.

Everything revolves around this preparation. Together with teammates at practice, I skate kilometer after kilometer at speeds I would never reach on my own. Day in, day out I skate single file with Simon Kuipers, Stefan Groothuis, and Jan Smeekens—each one of them world-class athletes in their distance events, but also people who understand that the real test is in the competition, not in the practice. Everyone makes their contribution to the team, and each month, each week, each day, the bar gets raised higher. And it's what I find the most fun: working with a team to bring out the best in each other. It's a lot more enjoyable and inspiring to be part of a synchronized team of skaters than in a free-for-all of egos.

It's what I look back on the most fondly. Of course, the day on the podium, the national anthem, and the nice bonus were wonderful, but the greatest feeling was bombing around a curve at sixty kilometers an hour with the best skaters in the world, my teammates, day after day.

Human society is like an arch, kept from falling by the mutual pressure of its parts.

~ Seneca

EXERCISE 4
DRONESHOTS OF YOUR LIFE

This visualization technique helps you put things in perspective.
You'll take a droneshot, as it were, of yourself. When you look down
at yourself from above, you can see that you're part of a
greater whole.

STEP 1 First read through the exercise, then find a comfortable seat and
close your eyes. Imagine that you're looking down at yourself from
a drone hovering right over your head.

STEP 2 The drone flies up to right above the house. Out loud, now ask
yourself, "What do I mean to this house? What do I mean to my family?"

STEP 3 The drone flies higher, so high now that you can see the whole
town. Ask yourself out loud, "What do I mean to this place?"

STEP 4 From the drone you can now see the entire country. Ask
yourself aloud, "What do I mean to this country?"

STEP 5 Now we're flying above the earth. Look down from
outer space. Ask yourself out loud, "What do I mean to
this planet?"

Zooming out gives you space, as well as time for
you to order your thoughts and for it to sink in
that you're part of a larger whole.

ACCEF

F

(AND

YOUR

TE

OVE IT)

Do not seek to have
events happen as you
wish, but wish them
to happen as they do
happen, and all will be
well with you.

~ Epictetus

Nobody wants to get sick, least of all athletes. Even the slightest cold can throw sand in the gears. Sniffing and coughing, you try to train anyway, because not practicing means falling behind on your training schedule. A day without training is a day without improvement, and as my competition isn't waiting around, sitting back means going backward. It's not all that crazy, then, that there once was a time when I viewed sick days as lost practice days.

I might have learned my lesson in 2002, when I lay overtrained on the couch, and I knew I had to slowly build my training intensity, but as an athlete you can't let yourself get too comfortable. To win, you need to push your boundaries, and that means balancing the limit of what your body can take. There's no safe route to gold. When in 2004, I wake up one day with a mild sore throat and a bit of a sluggish feeling, I try to ignore that too. There's a heavy session with timed intervals planned for today: six seven-minute blocks of hard laps. A crucial element in preparing for the world championship allround, which I want to win.

I am the reigning European all-round champion and world-record-holder in the big four (the 500, 1500, 5000, and 10,000 meters). Failing is not an option. I refuse to accept the situation and to listen to my body. I train all out. This only makes things worse: the cold turns into a flu, which then makes bringing home another win even harder. And being left home a whole lot easier.

Leading your life vs. being led

Deep down we all know that when push comes to shove, we're better off humbly bowing to nature. The natural philosophers preached riding life's natural waves long before Socrates and Zeno were born, and the Stoics continue down this same path, comparing our life course to a dog tied to the back of a cart.

The cart rumbles downhill, dragging the dog along. Do we run along and keep pace with life while enjoying the ride? Or do we resist, doing everything we can to stop the cart, and turn the trip into torture?

Epictetus teaches us to make the best of every situation, and not just that: he teaches us to love every situation. It's foolish and pointless to wish things were different than they are. For a start, it's simple logic—"wishing for figs in winter," he calls it. We can't deny life's reality.

Friedrich Nietzsche, the nineteenth-century German philosopher, wasn't a Stoic, and yet his life motto comes to the same thing as Epictetus's lessons: *amor fati,* or love your fate. Nietzsche thought this was the key to a happy life. The trick is not wishing things were different than they actually are. The dog that happily runs along with the cart isn't balking at being tied to a moving vehicle.

If you not only accept but even go so far as to love your fate, you'll be able to handle all of life. Obviously we can keep fighting against the natural course of events. However, that costs a lot of energy and eats away at our peace of mind, which is exactly what we don't want.

Nature can strike at any moment: floods, fires, drought—in antiquity these were common disasters. Seneca considers it a fact that these things will happen, and that it's up to us to gather the courage and resilience to deal with them as best we can. This is ideally done by harmonizing our judgment of these events with nature.

By this, Seneca means we're best off viewing disasters as natural phenomena. Rather than wishing they didn't happen to us, we can make the choice to get through them with courage and resilience. I'll show you a technique for doing that in the exercise at the end of this chapter.

Bibian Mentel

We can find a shining example of courage and resilience in Bibian Mentel, a Dutch snowboarder. Just as she was storming the top of the world rankings, fate struck: a large cancerous tumor was found in her lower leg.

When it became clear that her leg would have to be amputated, she made a conscious decision. Her leg would be removed, but during the conversation with the surgeon she resolved to look into what she could do with a prosthetic.

Four months later she was back on her board. She not only succeeded in promoting snowboarding to a Paralympic sport, but also won three gold medals. And even more impressive: she continued to live fully, even when she knew her life was coming to an end.

If anyone had the right to complain it would have been her. However, she lived according to Marcus Aurelius's words: "If something is difficult for you to accomplish, do not then think it impossible for any human being; rather, if it is humanly possible and corresponds to human nature, know that it is attainable by you as well." In other words, with the attitude you elect, with the way you choose to think, you can achieve an extraordinary amount.

Somehow, we expect there to exist a kind of natural scale that balances out our troubles. Having suffered pain or injustice, we might think we have a right to redress by doing someone else just the same.

THE STOIC FRIEND

We often think we're helping our friends by giving them advice, even when it's unsolicited. A friend will, however, benefit more from support, a listening ear and good questions. Here we can turn to a conversation technique developed by Socrates, one of the Stoics' great role models. The trick in a Socratic dialogue is to wholly omit your own opinion, and to only ask questions as factually as possible based on the other person's answers.

My greatest conversations with friends have come about when we've explored dilemmas and distilled questions from them. "How can you be successful *and* experience a sense of calm?" This question arose when I asked a good friend of mine about his dilemmas. Despite the fact that his answer ("success is when others find me successful") surprised me, I tried to respond with (Socratic) questions, without judging him and without advising him. While this felt unnatural, it did lead to a deeper conversation.

Or we might think "the world has to treat me nicely because I deserve it," or "my plan has to go exactly as imagined because I'm running the show." But this can lead to toxic thoughts such as "I'm never allowed to make mistakes."

These are all stories we tell ourselves, and we know they're wrong when we actually take the time to think them through. They're yet another example of what the Stoics meant by emotions resulting from wrong judgments, as discussed in chapter 2.

That is, by the way, not to say there's no place for emotions such as sadness, grief, or loss. It just means you have the choice to remain a victim of that sadness in the long term or not. *Amor fati* means learning to love reality, no matter how difficult that may be.

In the modern era it appears more and more often as though we're able to bend our fates to our wills. We have a cure for every complaint, a cash printer to regulate our economies, and the sidewalk tiles are seldom uneven.

We try to organize our lives like schedules. Everything gets filled in: who picks up the kids at what time, an afternoon get-together with friends, when and where we're going on vacation next year.

That's why it's growing harder for us to put up with uncertainty and chaos. It nevertheless remains a useful attitude toward life to see the charm in this absurd need to plan. Before you know it, life gets in the way. And you're better off laughing at the arbitrariness that life brings, giving yourself over to everything outside your power and understanding that fortune can also bring new opportunities.

From the flu to guitar

Wim den Elsen, an experienced trainer and household name in the speed skating world, was the one who taught me: "See sick days as natural rest days." "That's it!" I thought. It's self-delusion to think I'll never run up against the flu. To keep resisting it is counterproductive, even.

We're better off accepting that little flu as the natural course of events and resting. Often, however, we ignore it. We push through and for as long as we can still somewhat manage, we refuse to cancel any appointments, despite knowing better. Apparently it's hard to admit to ourselves that we need rest, and even harder to actually take a rest and sit around without feeling guilty about unfinished business and about that meeting we had to cancel. It's better to grab our chance to rest and, importantly, to enjoy it while it lasts.

"You're training hard enough, Mark," I told myself. "Take a step back for a moment and listen to your body. The sooner you recognize the signals, the better."

In the winter of 2002, when I was overtrained, I learned to play the guitar. I wasn't allowed any strenuous activities and so, to make the most of it, I taught myself to noodle. Making music activates nearly every area of your brain simultaneously, improving the cooperation between both halves.

Unwittingly, I was training in another way. I was literally playing to myself, enjoying myself. No right or wrong, goals or slumps—simply getting lost in the music. Playing guitar was a great mental distraction and far more useful than worrying or lingering in my frustrations.

Accepting situations for what they are doesn't come naturally to me. It feels particularly *unnatural* to accept those things obstructing the way to my goal. I will struggle, I will fight, I won't give up. It's the nature of the beast, I guess.

Only, it would be a ridiculous fight if in the process I ended up hurting myself more and as a result enjoying things even less. In that case, acceptance is a much better strategy. So I try to accept that life doesn't always go my way, and when possible, with a smile on my face.

You can only find peace after realizing that this fight against your fate is actually a fight against yourself. What you can't change, you have to accept—there's no other choice. If you want to be happy and find fulfillment, then you're left with one final step: to love your fortune. It's damn hard, but far from impossible.

Not "This is a misfortune" but "To bear this worthily is good fortune."

~ Marcus Aurelius

EXERCISE 5
EVERY DISADVANTAGE HAS ITS ADVANTAGE

The heart of the Stoic mindset, for me, is about accepting that things will go as they will. This exercise will help you not just to accept your fate but to love it.

STEP 1 Grab a sheet of paper and in one sentence at the top, nice and big, describe a situation that's bothering you. It can be anything, as long as it's something you can't change yourself.

⤳ "I'm not a pro soccer player and can't ever be one anymore."

STEP 2 In one sentence write what the most ideal solution for your problem would be.

⤳ "I make my debut in the MLS (Major League Soccer) at the age of forty-five."

STEP 3 Bad news: it ain't gonna happen. Never. Now imagine fully accepting that situation for what it is. Try to be as concrete as possible: what does full acceptance entail?

⤳ "When watching soccer on TV, I'll stop telling my friends and family that I'd have done things better."

STEP 4 Now note down at least ten advantages—there need to be *at least* ten!—of the situation as it now stands.

⤳ "If I'd been a pro soccer player, I probably wouldn't have had my family."

Can you embrace the advantages of the current situation? Do you perhaps see any new opportunities?

LESSON
6

DEATH
MAKES
LIFE
EPIC

Let us go to our sleep
with joy and gladness;
let us say: I have lived;
the course which Fortune
set for me is finished.

~ Seneca

Early one Sunday, a rest day for me, I light the fire basket. It's beautifully sunny out, and the flames crackle in a brisk breeze. Then a phone call suddenly disturbs the tranquility. It's my younger brother. Strange time of day, I think to myself. I answer and can hear from his voice that something is wrong. My mother is no longer with us—she took her own life.

Devastating though it is, the news doesn't surprise me. This wasn't her first attempt. My mother had suffered from depression for years and often said she no longer wanted to live. She didn't see another way out.

Over the years I regularly experienced feelings of incomprehension and anger, and at first I really struggled with what I saw as her giving up on life. How was that possible? Life was amazing, wasn't it? Our daughter had just been born, her first grandchild. She must have had so much to live for, surely?

But clearly she couldn't see, let alone feel that way. Maybe it's for the best that I can't understand it: what remains is the loss of my beloved mother who dedicated her life to her children.

Death as motivation for (a good) life

Death is an important subject within Stoic philosophy. Seneca wrote a lot about it: he was an advisor to Emperor Nero (37–68 AD) and had little certainty in life. Nero steadily revealed himself to be a cruel dictator during his reign, and even had his own mother murdered. A high position in the imperial court was then not the best guarantee for a long and peaceful life.

When in his old age Seneca retired to enjoy his pension, he reflected a great deal on his life. He shared the lessons he drew by, among other things, writing letters to his friend Lucilius.

In one of these letters, Seneca wrote that dying was an everyday process, as with each passing day another part of us was taken. With every day that we live, we come one step closer to death, even though we might not realize it. In that sense, death isn't something to be too grave about.

Despite being retired, Seneca didn't escape Nero's cruelty. He's found complicit in a plot to assassinate the emperor, for which Nero granted him the dubious honor of taking his own life. When the Roman legionaries knocked at Seneca's gate with the order, he didn't resist but decided with a sound mind to turn his death into a kind of theater performance. He breathed his last breath in a steaming bath, his wrists slit and a cup of poison empty.

What is death? Nothing more than no longer being here. Most Stoics don't believe in an afterlife, and through their way of thinking they give death the middle finger.

When Alexander the Great, the famous warlord with his boundless ambition, and his stable boy were dead, Emperor Marcus Aurelius told himself death doesn't distinguish between an emperor and a person without social status. For an autocrat like Marcus Aurelius—whose empire stretched from Scotland to Iran—this wisdom was an effective remedy against arrogance.

"I have to die," Epictetus used to say in his lectures. "If it is now, then I die now; if later, then now I will take my lunch, since the hour for lunch has arrived—and dying I will tend to later." A better, more disdainful wink at death is virtually unthinkable, provided you also really manage to maintain that attitude at the supreme moment.

Seneca repeats to himself: the definitive test to see whether I've lived well is still coming. By this he means he's always spoken great, wise words about how to deal with death, but that he can only make good on them at the end. Only then can we look back and give a truly honest answer to the question: have I lived as I wanted to? Only then will we know for sure whether such nonchalance about death was bravado or not. Or whether, as Seneca asks, "Am I merely saying brave sentiments, or do I really feel them?" Dying well means looking back without regret and is, above all, an encouragement to live well.

In any case, the Stoics did their best to die well and heroically. Since they're all dead anyway, I'm willing to venture that the death tales of Stoicism's big names are somewhat exaggerated here and there. Tradition would have it that Zeno found his improbable end when he walked out of his school, stumbled, and broke his toe. He took this as his sign it was time to die and, beating his arm on the ground, yelled, "I come of my own accord; why call me thus?" before dying where he lay—by holding his breath.

His successor Chrysippus allegedly died in a fit of laughter. An image of a drunk donkey eating twigs finished him off, apparently. Another reading is that he died while drunk after an Olympic banquet. From experience, I can tell you this version is more realistic: those parties can indeed get quite out of hand.

Of course we have to take these stories with a pinch of salt. I see them as a way of showing a total disdain for death—a kind of confirmation that truly great minds can die well and not be grave about it.

"Dying is easy. Everyone can do it," said René Gude, a Philosopher Laureate of the Netherlands who preferred the Stoics, right before his own death.

Don't let yourself be led by life

All things considered, it is of course absurd too that everything we cherish, everything we are, will at some point no longer be here. We are a small dot in the universe, nothing at all.

Rather than a sad fact, we can also see this as a valuable understanding. It ensures we spend our time on this earth well. Death is an outcome to the life of now, the life of today. We can find proof of that attitude in the reflections of people who find themselves at death's door.

Bronnie Ware, a caregiver who worked with dying people, asked them what, looking back on their lives, they regretted, and went on to write the book *The Top Five Regrets of the Dying*. The number one regret? "I wish I'd had the courage to live a life true to myself, not the life others expected of me"—a lesson to really get in our heads. This chapter's exercise can help you with that.

The understanding that every one of us will die is the best incentive to avoid regret. When you realize that the end could be close at hand—and that goes for everyone, every day—you also understand that you have an important choice to make daily: Are you spending your time on things you find valuable? Or are you letting yourself be carried away by choices you will regret when on your deathbed?

In this chapter's exercise you'll learn to think deliberately with death in view. We'll focus on the precious limited time we still have, to ensure you're more conscious of that time. Often we spend it on yet another hour of staring at our phone or TV screens, while after a good chat with a friend we conclude we should do that more often. But do we actually go and do it?

Why do we cling to our being right in an argument when we can let go of that anger, bringing us peace of mind sooner? Why don't we take a little time each day to breathe and go out in nature, instead of pushing through, being busy, or letting ourselves be carried along by the latest news? If we allow ourselves to be led by the issues of the day, by our impulses, are we using our time the way we really want to? Do we understand our time is finite?

With firm strokes over the natural ice

Sadly, my mom didn't pass away in 2012 with her head held high—that's what depression can do to you. It is a debilitating, sometimes deadly disease. Fortunately, there are enough people who do see light at the end of the tunnel with their depression, often thanks to professional help. My mom never managed to, and saw no other way out of her life.

Yet the moment of my mom's death is not the worst part for me: the sad part for me is that she didn't live her life to the fullest until the end—that she, in part due to her disease, wasn't able to embrace life and to love. My mom didn't die on the day I got the call. My mom had been dying for the previous ten years.

One of the hardest choices I ever had to make was to tell my mom she was better off staying at home during the Vancouver Games. She was already suffering from depression and didn't always feel her best. The trip would have been too hard on her, and her presence would be too hard on everyone going along to support me, and on myself.

She thought it was very unfair of me, and it hurt her. My mom, from whom I'd received so much unconditional love, told me how unfair she thought it was that she couldn't be present. Obviously she was the first one I called when I won, but at that moment she was overcome not with happiness but with sadness for not having been there.

GOOD STOIC RESOLUTIONS

Every year we promise ourselves to do new things, adding even more items to the long list of resolutions we didn't get around to doing last year but now are really going to do. What would happen if we turned this around and instead asked ourselves what we wanted to do *less* of? We could spend more time and energy on things that help us move forward and really matter.

Personally, I think this is a challenging one: I pick things up quickly and get excited by big ideas. But I also know I'll run up against myself if I don't cut things out first. That's why at the end of the year I make a list of things I want to do less of. What can I outsource? What can I stop?

I can't imagine how it feels to not be able to experience the most profound moments of pleasure, but I have seen the effects. My mom could, by the way, roar with laughter and enjoy things too, though those moments grew rarer over the course of the ten years her depression lasted.

My mom's depression made me think about death as well as about my own life. Death itself isn't bad, though not having lived for fear of everything is. That's why I ask myself: am I leading the life I want to live?

Two weeks after my mom's passing, the Netherlands is blessed with a strong cold front, leaving thick black ice everywhere: the dream and first love of every ice skater.

I've been left out of the selection for the coming tournaments but do have to be on standby as a reserve for the final World Cup competition. I'm also putting a lot of time into finding a new sponsor for our team, which is no easy task in the middle of an economic crisis.

With all of this in mind, I know it's unwise to skate on natural ice since there's a high chance of injury, but if I don't head out onto the lakes and canals now, I'll forever regret it. This is the reason I first started skating. This is, for me, back to nature, back to my roots.

I put on my skates and with firm strokes wind my way across the sweeping, frozen waters of the Weerribben, a nature reserve at the mouth of the IJssel River, where I first learned to skate as a little boy. The frosted reeds along the canals form a fairy-tale setting. I let the worries about whether we'll ever find a sponsor and how I, as an Olympic champion, might compete for prizes again someday drop away.

I've lost my mom, damn it! But I'm alive, I'm blessed with my family around me, and I'm skating. I skate under the rising sun with a stubborn, broad grin. This is glorious!

With death in mind, it's easier to define what's important to you. If you reflect for a bit daily on the fact that this day could be your last, are you at peace with the life you're leading?

We die every day, for every day some part of life is taken from us.

~ Seneca

EXERCISE 6
MINIMIZING REGRET

You're living life to the fullest when not having any deathbed regrets. This exercise will help you with that.

STEP 1 Grab a pen and sheet of paper.

STEP 2 Imagine: you're really old but still in good health. It's your birthday and you're hosting a big garden party for all your friends and family.

STEP 3 The most important people in your life are sitting with you at the table. Think of and write down which three friends or family members those are.

STEP 4 Speeches are made in your honor. Write the three most important points from those speeches. They can be anything: your (good) character traits, results you achieved, or decisions you made.

STEP 5 The party is over and you're lying in bed. You let the last years pass in review and think: which decisions did I regret not making? Write three things down.

Back to today: what actions can you take now so that you won't have any regrets in your old age?

HAPPINESS
IS A
SIDE
EFFECT

He is a king who fears
nothing, he is a king who
desires nothing.

~ Seneca

As an athlete, you're happy when you win. Winning is all you're focused on, so when you achieve that goal, it feels amazing.

At the 2010 Olympic Games, I make it onto the stage; the national anthem is played for me; I am given a tribute by Willem-Alexander, the then–Dutch Crown Prince; and upon returning home I receive a second distinction from Queen Beatrix. I am hailed as a hero, and the world lies, at least for a moment, at my feet.

But once you've actually won, it's not long before your focus shifts to winning even more: that must feel even better! And if you do go on to win even more, you're not just a medal winner, you're on your way to becoming a legend. And that's the ultimate.

As an entrepreneur, you want to make a profit. When you make a profit, you then want to build up capital and keep growing, and when you've built up capital and your business is flourishing, you then want to invest in other businesses. When you . . . and when . . . then this . . . and when . . . It's never-ending.

In the summer of 2010, the period after my Olympic success, I read studies about how long the "high" of a gold medal might last. And guess what? On average, the high lasts about three months. After that, you return to a kind of base level of happiness and look toward the next kick.

And you betcha, after three months the world appears to keep turning past me too. I might get interviewed a little more frequently, but that's it, really. The sun rises and sets again. It's not like I get up every day with an Olympic medal around my neck and smile at myself in the mirror.

The euphoria has a limited shelf life, so that summer I grab my notebook back from the bookcase to make new plans. How perfect would it be if I could retain my title? No Dutch person has managed to do that in the 1500 meters. Now that would be truly legendary, and produce a truly lasting feeling of happiness. That's where happiness must be waiting, right? At the end of the road? But it never ends.

Success isn't the same thing as happiness

The Stoics, as we now know, aren't focused on an end product or result: they're exclusively concerned with the *process* that ultimately—hopefully—leads to a desired result. A Stoic strives for peace of mind under all circumstances, whether that result is achieved or not.

The Stoics observed not only themselves, but also the people around them—people who we might say have achieved statuses so many desire: emperors, wealthy businessmen, successful senators, and athletes. Stoics described how miserable these people often felt.

Seneca writes about Emperor Augustus, who longed for an empty agenda as consolation for all his toil, while yearning after the pleasant illusion he would live for himself one day. Seneca mentions the famous orator and consul Cicero, who, sitting in his villa as the power struggle between Caesar and Pompey over Rome unfolded, called himself "half free." These outwardly successful figures constantly complained of wanting more, not being free, or wishing for peace of mind.

There are countless Olympic champions for whom the gold medal hangs around their neck like a lead weight: something extra is forever expected of them.

There are entrepreneurs who, after selling their businesses, have no clue what to do with their money and time. Or a musician like Avicii, who despite all his fame as a DJ and all the money in the world died from a cocktail of drugs, alcohol, and stress. We could label these people as "successful," and that should entail a sense of happiness. Or at least that's how a lot of us define happiness: in terms of money, fame, or success. But that is exactly what Stoic happiness is not.

Stoics strive for *eudaimonia*, which amounts to a state of inner calm and self-development regardless—and this is crucial—of one's circumstances. So we don't measure Stoic happiness against the absence of pain on the one side and as much pleasure or satisfaction as possible on the other.

No, eudaimonia is about growth, flourishing and finding meaning in life. It means growing and flourishing precisely by overcoming things. By learning to deal with pain, sadness, and other challenges while maintaining the same state of mind under all conditions. That is a happy life in the Stoic sense.

It's not for nothing that the Stoics hold in such high regard somebody like Socrates, who, as a philosopher, would never lose his composure in a debate. Or for Diogenes, the Cynic, who stubbornly made the point he didn't need much: he lived inside a barrel.

Seneca was a little more practical by nature. He believed it's okay to be quite rich, which he was, if you can also genuinely detach yourself from those possessions. Now, how can you enjoy your wealth if you're trapped by your fear of losing it? Seneca thought. Who rules over whom? Your possessions rule over your state of mind, rather than the other way around.

Eudaimonia, then, is more of a state of being, a mindset, than an end goal. If you are striving for the good, develop yourself—you'll have the greatest chance of finding peace of mind, independent of external results. Zeno defined happiness as a "good flow of life, with virtue," an independent form of happiness—independent of other people's states of mind and independent of one's possessions.

According to the Stoics, happiness is, in itself, a bad goal to aim for. That's because we don't find happiness at the finish line, but along the way.

The quote "It's not the destination, it's the journey" remains a favorite cliché among backpackers for good reason. They aren't just happy when finally reaching the hostel's bunk room. It's about the journey, even when it isn't exactly (or at all) smooth or enjoyable.

Stronger yet: the more we have to fight for something, the more meaning we attach to it and the more satisfaction we get out of it. The more hours we put into our studies and the harder the assignments are, the prouder we are of our results. The degree of happiness is thus determined by the time and energy we stick to something. By doing so we create meaning, and this meaning is unique for everyone.

For many people, happiness has to do with success and with desires and goals they want to achieve. I know incredibly wealthy people who are extremely restless and people with practically no money who don't see a single obstacle to doing what they like. The trick is on the one hand being able to set high goals, and on the other hand managing to maintain our inner peace.

Aren't you Mark Tuitert, that speed skater?

In the summer after my Olympic success, I'm brimming with expectation. As an Olympic champion I'm sure to be signing big sponsorship deals and dazzling in flashy commercials for Nike, Puma, or Adidas. The eternal search for a sponsor will soon be over.

The truth is I have to settle for less. It's 2010, and the economic crisis is at its deepest. Sponsors are by no means lining up. Our previous

THE STOIC PERFORMER

Whether you're a CEO, manager, coach, musician, stand-up comedian, or athlete, when you're onstage (or in a stadium) all eyes are focused on you. That understanding can carry a lot of pressure. Usain Bolt, the Jamaican Olympic track champion, never appears to experience pressure before his races. He waves to the crowd or messes around with the volunteers behind the starting block. I can assure you, though, he definitely feels that pressure but has learned to deal with it.

My recipe was to crack jokes with our physical therapists right before important races. It allowed me to set my thoughts, be it for just a few seconds, on another track. In this way I disengaged myself from the moment that was creating all this pressure. It's how you control your emotions, instead of the other way around.

sponsor, a local bank, went bankrupt the year before—so Olympic champion or not, it's back to having to look for yet another sponsor. My private dream of cool sports ads and big deals ends up being a commercial for Kinder Bueno, the popular chocolate candy bar, in which a woman addresses me with a "Hey, aren't you Mark Tuitert, that speed skater?" An ever-so-slight difference between my dream and reality.

I'm wrestling with myself as an Olympic champion, attaching all kinds of things to this label, as though I've become someone else. The reality is: I won a nice title and got an amazing result—but this result is also separate from who I am, at heart still that boy from the village of Holten who was crazy about speed skating.

This realization only sinks in a few days before the Olympic qualifiers in Sochi, in December 2013. By then, Gerard van Velde has been my coach for almost two years. He himself won Olympic gold in an extraordinary way in 2002. He'd been among the world's best for years but had yet to win a big international title, until at the end of his career he threw all caution to the wind and showed what he was really made of. If there's anyone who knows what's going on inside my head, it's him.

For weeks I've been skating below my level, and it's gnawing at my peace of mind. I struggle with my routine—I've trained super hard but am failing to get results. At a world cup race in Berlin in November, I finish at the back of the pack. On the eve of the Olympic qualification tournament at the end of December 2013, it crosses my mind: this might just be my last race—I'm miles away from holding onto my Olympic title. I decide to discuss these doubts with my coach.

Gerard opens my eyes: "Mark, you're thirty-three years old, already an Olympic champion, a father, and you've worked so hard to get here. Cherish that, and be proud of it. You have nothing to lose—enjoy the coming tournament."

That day I drive home from the ice rink with tears in my eyes. He's right. The lessons I've learned, the fulfillment I get, coupled with the inner peace resulting from it, feel like a state of deeper happiness. I have grown, have experienced a lot, have gotten to know both sides of the medal, and all together it's made me who I am.

It's exactly this calm that ensures I start the Olympic qualifier tournament with the right mindset. I have nothing to lose and don't think about the result. If this turns out to be my last race, I will go down fighting if anything.

I grow over the course of the tournament and grab my chance in the very last round of the last race of that weekend: I win the 1500 meters and qualify for the Sochi Games.

Happiness lies in rising to the challenge, in wrestling and growing. In improving, doing the right thing, learning, and by way of all this, finding inner calm. That's an important part of eudaimonia and goes much further than a golden medal, riches, or status. Happiness isn't an end goal, it's a byproduct of the journey there.

Wherever I go it will be well with me, for it was well with me here, not on account of the place, but of my judgments which I shall carry away with me, for no one can deprive me of these; on the contrary, they alone are my property, and cannot be taken away, and to possess them suffices me wherever I am or whatever I do.

~ Epictetus

EXERCISE 7
GRATITUDE EXERCISE

The best recipe for becoming happier is to increase your gratitude.
By doing so, you focus automatically on what you do have,
rather than on what you don't.

STEP 1 Grab a piece of paper (or a nice notebook) and a pen, and
lay them next to your bed.

STEP 2 Before you turn the light off tonight, write three things
you're thankful for today. This can be big (your partner's love) but
also small (that your pillow is comfy).

Do you like this exercise? Do it again tomorrow!

LESSON
8

A

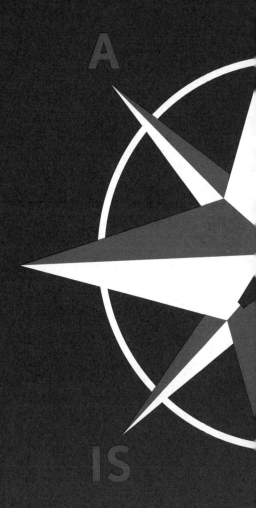

IS

GOOD,

COMPASS

BETTER

If one knows not to which port they sail, no wind is favorable.

~ *Seneca*

If Seneca had seen the way I muddled along after life as a professional athlete, he'd have raised his eyebrows.

When I was still skating, I had a clear goal in the Olympic Games, a clear North Star by which to adjust my coordinates. It'd been set years earlier, including the date and time. I knew exactly at which moment I needed to peak, when I needed to push myself, during which weeks I had to rest, and how my team of colleagues would look. But after that, when the skates had been hung up? I had no idea, I just did whatever.

In order to explore what life after my skating career will look like, I drink coffee with every Tom, Dick, and Harry in the hope that someone can tell me what I have to do.

I wander around my house like a headless chicken. My wife and I have just moved, with two young kids. I'm living in a new environment, no longer close to the ice rink where I always had to perform. I abruptly find myself living without a team, without a goal, without a destination or direction.

A good friend then offers me some advice: "Mark, you need to get out and work. You don't know what that is." Pardon? I don't know what work is? I trained twice a day for fifteen years, and you're telling me I "don't know what work is"? Putting my initial indignation aside, I decide to follow his advice and start applying to jobs. In one of my first interviews I get asked what I'm good at. "Skating laps counterclockwise," I joke. I genuinely don't know. So there I am at an office, in a smart shirt, and all around me are potential colleagues who apparently know exactly what they're doing. All kinds of questions flash through my mind: Who am I? What do I want? What can I do?

Where is that goal I always had so clearly in mind? I see people around me starting companies, getting promoted, earning degrees, and finding their passion in the profession they practice. I'm looking for a clear map that will point the way to a clear goal. But where do I find that?

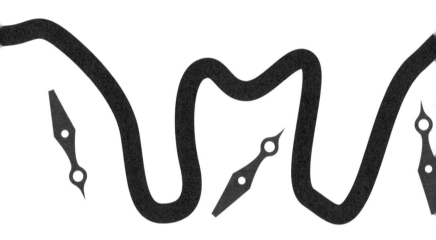

You'll find your own path to your goal

Seneca wrote a lot about finding the right direction. He marveled at people who just muddled along, not knowing what they wanted and meanwhile complaining that nothing was working.

According to Seneca, you have to think carefully about what you want to do with your life but in the meantime take action: "the one does not exist apart from the other: the one man cannot live in contemplation without action, nor can the other act without contemplation." By this he means that it's good to think about where you want to go before heading out, and that you can only know whether you're on the right track once you actually set out.

Think about the way you navigate on Google Maps: it's only when you start walking that you know whether you're heading the right way. It's the same in life. You navigate slowly and by way of unavoidable

detours toward your goal. You sail a stretch, stop to check whether you're still going the right way, adjust the course if necessary, and continue. So the route never takes a straight line to your goal, across a calm sea or down a beautiful, paved highway.

For the Stoics, it's not about reaching the harbor but about the sailing itself. When you're bobbing in the middle of an ocean, a harbor can feel incredibly far away. That's why it's important that you also define a direction, a route. How are you going to reach that harbor?

When searching for this route, we often have the tendency to do the same as others. We cling to the same map used by everyone else and follow the herd like meek sheep rather than searching for our own path.

Everyone will doubt their route at times, and then it can feel safe to wander down well-worn paths. For example, you can "just" produce chocolate with another flavor, or you can be like Ben & Jerry's, the popular ice cream brand that also promotes fair trade practices and supports better treatment and acceptance of refugees.

As an ice skate designer, you can take the classic long track skate as your model, or you can experiment: what if you separated the blade from the heel and turned the connection at the front into a hinge? You then end up with a "clap skate," which helped skaters rip the world records to shreds during the nineties.

If it worked for others, then it'll certainly do so for you too. According to the Stoics, this line of reasoning is a pitfall: it's essential to find a path that aligns with your nature, to not let yourself get distracted by what others expect of you, to not let yourself get carried away by what the majority thinks.

That this route might be difficult, and doesn't have any of the well-known accommodations or refuges, is part of it. That's why it's better to have a compass than a map. Rather than looking for the perfect route, you can decide the direction. It's precisely through this searching for the right direction that we find our own way and dare to do what suits us.

Doing what suits us is a duty, according to Marcus Aurelius. He reproaches us when we get out of bed with reluctance and don't do what we were born to do. Don't you see the ants, plants, sparrows, spiders, and bees? They are all doing, in their way, their jobs in the cosmos—and you don't want to get up to do your work as a human being? Not do what aligns with your nature? Then you really don't care about yourself, Marcus Aurelius thought.

As a child, Marcus Aurelius was a diligent philosophy student. He would have certainly become a philosopher if he hadn't been chosen early on by Hadrian, the then-emperor, who didn't have children of his own, to succeed him.

Just imagine that: you're completely ready to follow your nature and become a philosopher, when as a child the highest function in the world is thrust onto you. The young Marcus Aurelius also had trouble getting accustomed to the practices of the imperial court, where injustice and corruption were rampant. The Roman empire was a dictatorship where succession to the throne wasn't always considered. The families of previous emperors were regularly murdered, and once emperors secured power, they tried to maintain it no matter the cost.

Nevertheless, Marcus Aurelius made the emperorship his own by following his nature and applying his philosophical lessons while holding the highest function. He told himself: "No matter where you might live, you can lead a good life. Now, you might live at the court, so you can lead a good life at the court as well."

Marcus Aurelius used his aptitude for philosophy and his calm character to become a good leader. By bringing his aptitude and his training in line with his duty—we might also call it his fate—to lead the Roman empire, he still managed to fulfill his own potential, and by doing so to be the first and perhaps only philosopher-emperor.

Find your compass

In particular it's the younger people I meet who speak about "doing good for the world"—about meaningfulness. They set themselves big goals like saving the world and fighting injustice, though these goals remain abstract and far off. Think then, above all, about how you want to achieve your goal. Otherwise you run the risk of having serious motivation issues when after a few months of work you feel like you still haven't made any progress. The gap between that goal and your daily reality can be so wide that your motivation vanishes and you throw in the towel.

So forget for a second the meaning of *purpose*, which has become a buzzword. Forget describing a big goal. Forget following your passion. You'll discover those passions and those goals after first establishing your direction.

The trick is doing what aligns with your nature, is finding that problem you aren't forced to face but above all want to wrestle with every day. Something you would also do if, at least in the short term, you weren't paid to do it. That which we do every day determines who we become. That's where fulfillment lies: in the work of every day.

It's only been two years since hanging up my skates, and I've tried a lot of different things. I've learned what I don't want, what I can't do, and what doesn't suit me. I didn't find that out by reading even more and thinking carefully in an easy chair but instead by going out and doing.

I worked at a temporary recruitment and work agency, organized my own bike race, and set up a business to sell specialist ice skates, but nothing yet that fits all my facets. I have a feeling I need to go back to the drawing board, to lie at anchor for a while to redetermine my direction and adjust my compass.

Rob, my younger brother, comes to my rescue. He tells me how he found his own direction by sticking to his nature. He draws a triangle with an area of interest at each point, like the coordinates of a compass. His natural interests are:

♦ Music. Give him an instrument and he'll play any song he hears.
♦ Games. He loves to play games, and even as a kid he used to come up with challenging mazes for DeeDee, our hamster. Poor animal.
♦ Technology. He wants to understand how things are made and how to do them himself.

In daily life Rob designs interactive playground equipment. I've never heard him complain, and he always speaks lovingly about his profession. I want the same. I know that feeling very well from my skating career, but I need to find it again.

On my own compass I fill in:

♦ Autonomy. I would really like to choose my own path and be my own boss. Plus, I don't mind taking risks. It's no surprise that I'm drawn to entrepreneurship.

- Sports. I've been athletic from a young age and have built up knowledge surrounding that. I can't imagine a life without sports.
- Philosophy. I'm a thinker and trying to understand life. I present, write, read, and take time to think about life.

AUTONOMY **PHILOSOPHY**

SPORTS

In everything I now do, these elements are present. In every role I fulfill, these are my coordinates and everything I take on falls within my triangle. And the points reinforce one another: I philosophize ultimately to make better decisions, while my Stoic mindset helps steady my direction as an athlete and entrepreneur. I like using sports as a metaphor and inspiration.

For me, my brother's model connects nicely with what I've learned from the Stoics and other classical philosophers. The Stoics emphasize living in accordance with nature: you can only interpret that very broadly, so broadly that it's easy to forget what this means in concrete terms.

In my interpretation of the Stoic mindset, the emphasis lies on self-development and action. Thinking is always done in service of doing. Zeno was a merchant and philosopher. Chrysippus was an athlete, scientist, writer, and philosopher. Seneca was a consul, writer, and philosopher, while Marcus Aurelius was an emperor and philosopher. Stoic philosophy is what unites them—beyond that,

THE STOIC STUDENT

Studying isn't a competition to show how brilliant you are compared to others. It's a pathway to expand your toolbox for life. When you find fulfillment in learning itself, you cultivate a growth mindset for the rest of your life.

A Stoic will never assume they're the wisest but instead always be searching, and in that sense they're a lifelong student. With that as my starting point, I launched the podcast *Drive*. I wanted to learn how to interview people and ask better questions, so I started speaking with driven coaches, artists, athletes, scientists, and entrepreneurs about their motivations.

they're completely different people with different goals and different talents. The Stoic mindset doesn't offer you a set map for a meaningful life, then, but a compass by which to take steps in the right direction, to improve them along the way and to find your own direction.

Sometimes this can feel lonely: nobody can truly understand you or walk a mile in your shoes. I too got advice from plenty of people, but in the end that first conscious step in my own direction really had to be set by myself. That's our own responsibility, to establish our own direction and to take the first step.

When choosing your own direction, you'll discover what you enjoy and what gives you fulfillment so that success truly becomes your own. Of course, my compass's coordinates aren't set in stone, and they can change over time, like a flowing river that never stays the same, but essentially they provide the basis for my life strategy.

I hope the following exercise helps you choose your own direction, a direction that suits your nature.

First say to yourself what you would be; and then do what you have to do.

~ Epictetus

EXERCISE 8
THE LIFE DIRECTION TRIANGLE

So you're still struggling to define your own direction. How do you choose one? With the help of this exercise, you will learn what suits your character, what brings you joy and pleasure, and where your interests lie: enter the Life Direction Triangle.

STEP 1 Grab a sheet of paper and draw a triangle. Make it big, as you'll need to be able to write inside it.

STEP 2 Come up with three words that define you the most. To help you out: think of one that fits your character, one that brings you joy or pleasure, and one that you find interesting. Write your answers at each of the triangle's three corners.

STEP 3 Now which words come to mind that satisfy all three of the answers you gave in step 2? Keep them as general as possible: these can be professions or businesses but also actions, plans, or ideas.

STEP 4 If you think of something that only meets one or two of the answers, write it outside the triangle: these are hobbies you can do in your free time. Maybe you're very interested in soccer, are made happy by it but aren't exceptional at it—that's an ideal hobby.

Of course, the words at the corners of this triangle might change. You can get better at something or lose interest. Repeat this exercise every couple of years.

CHARAC
MOST IMPO

CHARACTER

CHARACTER

CHARACTER

CHARACTE

CHARACTER

CHARACTER

CHARACT

CHARACTER

CHARACTER

CHARAC

CHARACTER

CHARACTER

CHARA

R IS YOUR
ANT PROJECT

CHARACTER	CHARACTER	CHARACTER	CHARACTER
CHARACTER	CHARACTER	CHARACTER	CHARACTER
CHARACTER	CHARACTER	CHARACTER	CHARACTER
CHARACTER	CHARACTER	CHARACTER	CHARACTER
CHARACTER			

Just that you do the right thing. The rest doesn't matter.

~ **Marcus Aurelius**

I'm on a soccer field with Tom, my young son. It's time for a mini game. Together with the boy from next door, who's even younger and smaller, I play against my son and daughter, the opposition. Normally putting those two on the same side is a recipe for arguments, but this time things are going well—until I pass the ball to our neighbor and he takes a shot at the goal where my daughter is playing goalkeeper.

She lets the ball roll through her legs. After all, things should be fun for everyone. Tom, though, is having none of it: blind with rage, he screams the place down. He wants to win, the little Caesar. I have to laugh at this little version of myself and attempt a losing-is-part-of-the-game speech, but without much success.

The beautiful thing about kids is that they react so immediately, though I wonder how I'm going to teach my son to not become his own worst enemy. How can I make him see that there's a balance to be struck between desiring to win and being a good person? Of course every dad will say this, but still: he's already a fantastic little guy. But he's also very temperamental. I want to teach him what's important.

Aiming to equal the sage

One of the most important Stoic principles has to do with character. How do we cultivate good character? That is, I think, perhaps the most important question of Stoicism. Marcus Aurelius puts it nicely when he proposes that each day we should say to ourselves: "Today I shall be meeting with interference, ingratitude, insolence, disloyalty, ill-will, and selfishness—all of them due to the offenders' ignorance of what is good or evil." According to Marcus Aurelius, it's about being able to make that distinction yourself.

As an example of a good person, the Stoics use the idea of the sage, an archetypal hero. The sage is someone who leads a perfect life, in total harmony with nature, according to the highest of human values. They are the epitome of courage, temperance, justice, and wisdom, the cardinal virtues from classical philosophy. The word "cardinal" derives from the Latin word *cardo*, which more or less translates to "hinge." These values are seen as the hinge in life, a point around which everything else turns.

The cardinal virtues are character traits that everyone can develop to lead a good life. By that the Stoics don't mean what we now often understand by values: cleanliness, honesty, and decency. Being virtuous boils down to doing the right thing in daily life, for ourselves and for others. If you pursue the right virtues, you can flourish, you can grow into what you want to be.

You can't lead a good life in the Stoic sense if you don't propagate these cardinal values. The Greek Stoics were dogmatic on this: you either led a good life or a bad one. But over the centuries (and right up to today) Stoicism has developed a more practical and less rigid approach. The sage is the ideal, but as simple souls we are probably always going to be busy approaching that ideal. None of the Stoics, by the way, considered themselves to be sages. This high ideal remains unattainable for virtually everyone. But that doesn't mean we shouldn't strive for it.

Truly legendary figures are renowned for a lot more than just their achievements or victories. Muhammed Ali established himself as a champion for equal rights for Black Americans: for justice, then. It made him a unique character, an example, a legend.

Nelson Mandela fought courageously for the abolition of apartheid in South Africa, and in doing so, for equal rights for every citizen regardless of their skin color. He would pay a high price for his convictions: for twenty-seven years he was locked up and oppressed. Upon his release he showed the cardinal virtues of wisdom and temperance by taking a conciliatory attitude and striving for peace and freedom instead of personal redress for his suffering. Incidentally, Mandela had a copy of Marcus Aurelius's *Meditations* with him in his cell.

Almost every one of these heroes' good traits can be traced back to the following cardinal virtues:

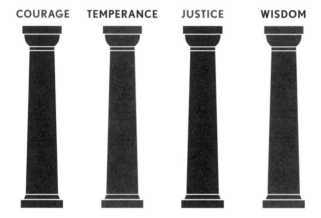

COURAGE   TEMPERANCE   JUSTICE   WISDOM

Courage to overcome the fear holding you back from taking action. The guts to swim against the stream. Courage to endure illness, loss, or a pandemic without giving in to complaint or to wishing things were different.

Temperance to know how much you truly need of something. Knowing when you have enough and are able to bring your life into balance and to regulate your emotions.

Justice to act rightly in relation to other people. Standing up for the weaker and being equally as nice to the secretary as to the CEO.

Wisdom to make the distinction between what is good and bad, what is right to strive for in everyday life and what is not.

If as an athlete you turn to doping, if as a parent you go swearing and cursing up and down the sidelines of the field, if as a politician you intentionally pit groups of people against one another, or if as a CEO you manipulate numbers to mislead shareholders, the Stoics would say you are doing the opposite and making every result worthless.

The All Blacks' cardinal virtues

When we get home from our little game I show Tom a video from the All Blacks, the New Zealand national rugby team. He loves the haka, an impressive traditional war dance performed by the team before every game. The stamping feet, powerful poses, and wild mouths do their work.

Much more important to me, however, are the team's core values: Better people make better All Blacks. Better people make better players. And not, it occurs to me, just better players, but also better entrepreneurs, better friends, and better fathers.

Wanting to win is great, I tell Tom. The All Blacks want the same, but they don't do so by being jerks. Playing a game is both to engage in battle and to accept the rules of the game with respect for everyone. It's more than a game to win or lose, it's a way of getting the most out of yourself.

For that you need an opponent at your level, the courage to enter the fray, the temperance or self-discipline to not let yourself get carried

THE STOIC LEADER

Stoic leaders make decisions based on guiding principles: the values they want to pass on to the people they are leading. A nice example is Marcus Aurelius's emperorship. Even though he, as the emperor of Rome, was an undisputed autocrat—perhaps the most powerful man on earth—his first deed was to seek rapprochement with the senate. His guiding principle was that he, as emperor, was there to serve society, represented by the senate, and he acted accordingly.

Stoic leaders don't do things to become popular—they become popular because they do the right things. They stay calm under substantial pressure and take others into account.

away by emotions on the field and instead to stay calm, the justice to fight according to the rules and respect every call, and the wisdom to know when you should give it your all and when someone else deserves it more—your much smaller neighbor, for example.

We need examples—a sage—to make a story understandable. In all areas, from sports to politics to business, there are individuals and teams demonstrating that success doesn't have to come at the expense of others and that character and values are essential parts of a good life. When we choose the right role models, we stand on the shoulders of giants—be their names Marcus Aurelius or the All Blacks. Building character is a never-ending project.

I see Tom laughing as he does the haka's final pose—the rest is material for later.

It is in the character of growth that we should learn from both pleasant and unpleasant experiences.

~ Nelson Mandela

EXERCISE 9
CARDINAL PILLARS

In order to train your good character traits, it helps to remind yourself of Stoicism's cardinal virtues every day.

STEP 1 Draw four pillars on a sheet of paper and write the following words above them:

Pillar 1: COURAGE
Pillar 2: TEMPERANCE
Pillar 3: JUSTICE
Pillar 4: WISDOM

STEP 2 Hang or place the sheet on a spot where you'll see it often, such as next to the mirror in the bathroom, next to your coffee machine, or on the wall next to your desk.

STEP 3 Set yourself a time period—this can be a week or a month—during which each day you will keep track of which cardinal virtues you have applied.

STEP 4 Take a moment at the end of each day to look back at the character traits you displayed. Set a checkmark in that pillar. You can of course use another system, as long as you make it visually evident that you're making progress.

Can you see, after a number of days, on which of the cardinal virtues you can still make progress? How might you work on that?

ACTIONS
SPEAK
LOUDER
THAN WORDS

We do not learn for school, but for life.

~ Seneca

The first successes I was able to claim during my teenage years weren't on ice but on asphalt. As a kid just turned seventeen, a career as a professional speed skater seemed a long way away, but in roller blades I could keep pace with the best seniors in the country.

In the summer after the 1997 Elfstedentocht ("Eleven Cities Tour"), the longest speed skating tour in the world and a Dutch national tradition, thousands of people lined the roads in the Netherlands to catch a glimpse of their ice-skating heroes demonstrating their skills, now in summer conditions, on wheels. In a duel in the streets of Apeldoorn, I beat the tour's number two, a national celebrity: Erik Hulzebosch. Maybe I would be able to win the Elfstedentocht someday.

That unfulfilled ambition resurfaced when I gave up professional skating. I was convinced I could extend my career a while longer in an "easy" way. I found a gap in my schedule between the time I was putting into my new job in the sales team at a temporary recruitment agency and into my family, and signed up for two ice sessions a week in Den Haag with the region's best marathon skaters. I'd quickly be able to compete with the nation's best, so as to have a shot at a spot among the famous racing pack at the Elfstedentocht—the ultimate dream for competition skaters, and for me.

But whereas at seventeen I'd breezed along with the best on rollerblades, I now slogged along anonymously at the back of the B peloton for the marathon. That's how a pair of well-trained amateurs and an old Olympic champion skated their laps on cold, wet ice rinks. Between my job, media appearances, and presentations, I tried to cram a couple more practice sessions into my schedule each week. More than enough, I thought, to be able to keep up with a peloton in any case.

I soon had a rude awakening, however, when I couldn't finish a single race and often had to give up halfway through. After a few races it was clear this wasn't going to be my ticket to the Elfstedentocht. There I was with all my knowledge of philosophy, training, and life, armed with a Stoic mindset, handed a serious reality check.

It's all about actions

In his lectures, Epictetus likes to use the example of an athlete training for the Olympic Games—which naturally appeals to me.

According to Epictetus, we must consult ourselves: what do we need to do to achieve something? A simple, but crucial question. We can say that we want to compete in the Olympic Games, but so do countless others. Of course it's still fantastic, a nice goal, but think of what it entails. You'll have to follow a diet, training schedule, and your trainer like they're your doctor.

You won't be able to drink wine to your heart's content; you'll also have to train when it's cold, or really hot; you'll have to do a lot and perhaps give up even more. You'll suffer injuries, pain; you'll have to wrestle through disappointments. It's hard work.

Carrying out is a totally different story than just wanting or imagining. Form an image of what's necessary to achieve something and ask yourself whether you're prepared to take those steps. Once you've done that, there's just one thing left: action.

That's exactly how the Stoics I've introduced practiced philosophy. Marcus Aurelius used a Stoic mindset to keep cool and deal with the responsibility pushed onto him of being a Roman emperor. He didn't write extensive philosophical treatises, just short notes to remind himself of the best way to look at daily problems. For him, philosophy is not some finalized theory but much more a living way

DO
SOMETHING

of thinking that has to be applied every day. Philosophy served as a basis for the choices he made. He followed it as best as he could and tried to demonstrate so with his deeds.

The Stoics aren't concerned with winning arguments, working out abstract theories, or, like scholars, searching for truth on paper. The value of philosophy lies in practice: the Stoic mindset centers on applying theory in an active life—in politics, as a parent, as a citizen, as a human being.

Armed with the right Stoic mindset, we can make better choices, getting to know ourselves and the world, through which we create a better basis for our actions. And it's those actions that demonstrate that we have digested the lessons properly. The Stoics continuously emphasize the value of actions over words. They carefully consider why they do something, and they don't orate about what they are going to do—no, they demonstrate it.

Epictetus makes the comparison with a carpenter. A carpenter doesn't say, "Let me tell you how I build houses." No, they take the assignment to build a house and show they are a master of their trade. Boasting about how good we are at something says nothing, except maybe that we're good at boasting. That's of no use to us at all. We have to show it.

Those who fail, learn

While an idea can appear so promising on paper, it's only when you execute it in the real world that you know whether it's genuinely a good idea or not. In my current career as an entrepreneur, the market is the

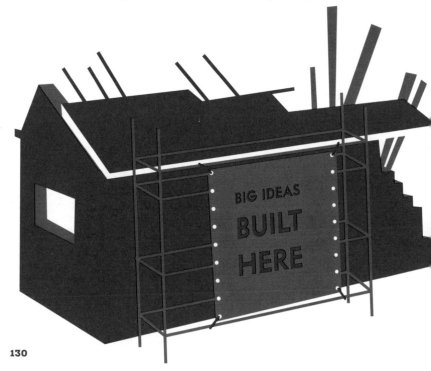

place where I test my ideas. I started by making a business plan and calculated everything out for the coming years to two digits after the decimal. But as nice as my plans were, as unique as my idea for caffeine chewing gum was, as flashy as my PowerPoint presentations or as sleek my sales pitch, it all came down to one question: was there a market for my product? That's an external factor I can do little to nothing about.

Testing our ideas consists of going out and researching whether our ideas hold water when exposed to external factors like the market. You have an idea, make a plan, and develop your product, then you test it in the market and learn how to sell it, after which you analyze, learn, and improve. How you tackle that process, which is full of failures and emotions, and how much energy you put into it is up to you. What's not up to you: the market.

We regularly kid ourselves by thinking we can do everything, while only really learning when we fall flat. It's the only way to learn—there's no way around it. That's why it's so important to train yourself in applying the right mindset, which helps you to deal more resiliently and flexibly with situations and to learn from them. It helps to understand that we sometimes have to give something up, that we have to say no and make choices.

Taking action with a Stoic mindset

Of course with my two training sessions a week I couldn't beat professional marathon skaters who were training two times a day to win the Elfstedentocht. How'd I ever get that into my head? Failure was not just a possibility—in this case it was a certainty.

Fortunately, failing isn't pointless. It confronts you with the questions: Do I really want this? What do I want and why? It's a test for your convictions.

THE STOIC YOUNG PROFESSIONAL

At twenty-one years old, I thought that as a talented skater I'd soon be an Olympic champion. That didn't happen until I was twenty-nine, relatively late in my career. By that time I enjoyed the process of performance itself much more than I necessarily needed the medal in hand.

If you haven't yet found your calling in work as a young professional or your expected success has been late in coming, remember that time is your dear friend. That doesn't mean, by the way, that you don't have to take action now. Spring into action but measure your results later down the line. Short-term action = long-term results.

You can't say you want something and at the same time not take the action necessary to achieve what it is you want. Then you're just fooling yourself, and you'll end up in conflict. Just like the athlete who wants to win Olympic gold but doesn't make it their task to live for that every day. You either want to achieve something and do what's necessary, or you don't want it. It's that simple.

That's also how I reach the decision to quit my job. I want to be an entrepreneur, I tell myself. That means I need to invest time and money, while keeping in mind that it can take years to build something profitable. I will have to persevere, invest, take courage, and work together with partners and clients. It's the ultimate test for my ideas.

Entrepreneurship is in that sense similar to professional sports. But that goes for everything done by people with the drive to achieve something. Maybe for another it's making a beautiful design, writing a striking text, or coming up with a bit of code that improves a computer program's functioning.

Finding that drive is a process of trial and error that can bring out heavy emotions because you're fully committing to something. You put a lot of yourself into it and have skin in the game.

Of course I sometimes don't see the point, of course I have my doubts, and that's why I have to tell myself over and over again that what I'm trying to achieve takes time, that patience and perseverance are needed.

The Stoic mindset helps remind you that in life things ultimately come down to one thing: yourself. Whether you're an entrepreneur or have a steady job, are a professional athlete, soldier, nurse, hairdresser, father, mother, son, daughter, partner, and/or friend; whether you win or lose, in good or bad times: you are the one who needs to act, to make choices.

No matter how great your plans might be, however you think you might be able to direct your life, your room to maneuver is limited. What you can do is concentrate on what's up to you and completely accept what lies beyond your power. In that way you can lead a fuller life, bringing the best out of yourself while staying true to yourself, regardless of the situation. The mindset developed by the Stoics to do so is thousands of years old. However, these same principles will still apply two thousand years from now.

Stoic philosophy offers a system of thinking that keeps us grounded in reality. By applying these ideas, we can guarantee our resilience and elasticity. We might be at the mercy of our fates, of chaos and unpredictability, but we can meet them with a grounded way of thinking and living that provides us direction in all circumstances and offers us peace of mind.

If you're on a sports field, go ahead and play to win. If you're building a business, go ahead and dream big. If you're doing research, go ahead and be ambitious. If you want to have a career, go ahead and aim for the top. Bring out the best in yourself, search for that drive that's deep down inside you. Give it your all, regardless of the actual result. If you can do that, you can't fail. Truly failing is to not try something for fear of the consequences of losing.

When you fail at something you think is great, you haven't lost anything. When you win at something you think is awful, you've won nothing. In life, it's not about whether you win or lose, but how you play the game.

Now in the school we are irritable and wordy; and if any little question arises about any of these things, we are able to examine them fully. But drag us to practice, and you will find us miserably shipwrecked.

~ Epictetus

EXERCISE 10
SHARING YOUR GOALS

Nothing works better to make sure you actually take action than telling someone else about your plans. You can approach that as follows:

STEP 1 Formulate your goal or what you want to achieve as concretely as possible. Concrete means within a set period of time and with a measurable outcome.
→ I want to read ten books in two months.

STEP 2 Which obstacles can keep you from achieving your goal? Try to think of them as concretely as possible.
→ I get distracted by my phone.
→ After work I'm too tired to read.

STEP 3 Think of a colleague, friend, or family member with whom you want to share your goals, somebody who's close to you and who isn't afraid to tell you the truth.

STEP 4 Email, text, or write a letter to them using the outline on the next page.

Dear _____ ,

I'm currently trying to achieve _____ .
I'll consider my plan successful when: (fill in your concrete goal and time)

_____

_____

_____

The problems I expect and the steps I have in mind to reach my goal

are:

• Obstacle 1: _____

_____

• Obstacle 2: _____

_____

• Obstacle 3: _____

_____

You'll help me a lot if in _____ days / months you check in with me
to ask how it's going and whether I've found ways to overcome these
obstacles.

Thanks,

_____

Notes

About the Author

MARK TUITERT won the gold medal in speed skating in the 1,500-meter event at the 2010 Vancouver Winter Olympics. After retiring from competitive speed skating, Mark has continued to make a positive impact as a bestselling author, successful entrepreneur with a global health and food business, host of the podcast *Drive*, motivational speaker, and representative for some of the largest organizations in the world. He has been featured on TED Talk and also serves as an on-air speed skating pundit for the Dutch broadcaster NOS. Mark is a husband and a father of two.